anythink

D0583576

NO LONGER PROPERTY OF
ANYTHINK LIBRARIES/
RANGEVIEW LIBRARY DISTRICT

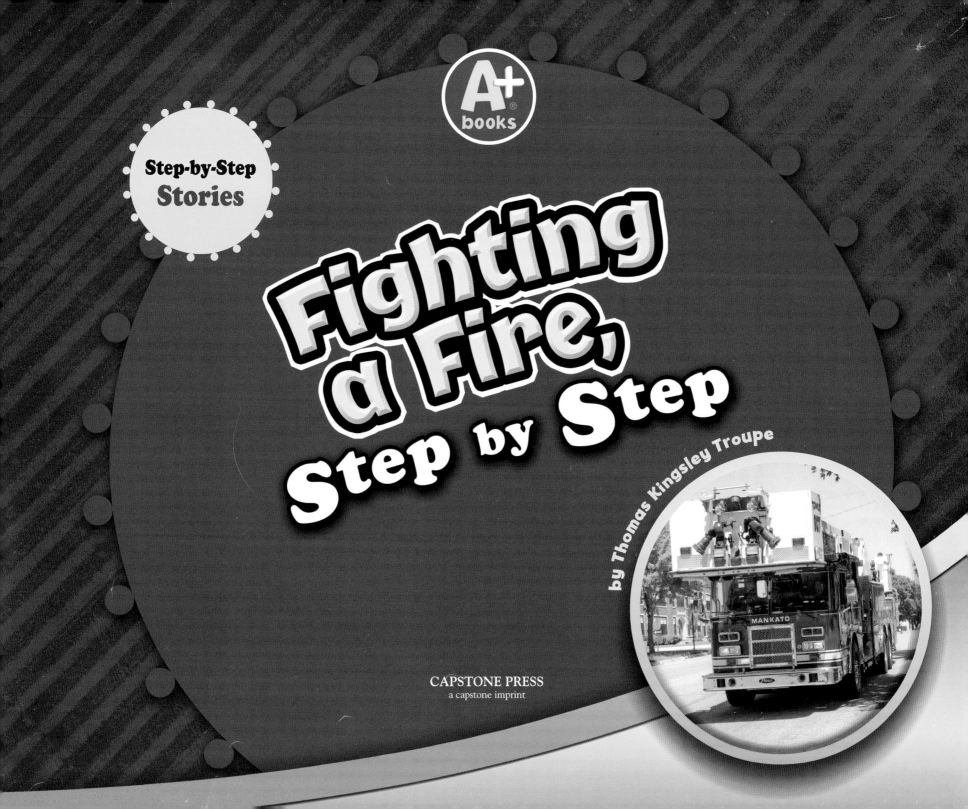

A+ books

Step-by-Step Stories

Fighting a Fire, Step by Step

by Thomas Kingsley Troupe

CAPSTONE PRESS
a capstone imprint

A+ Books are published by Capstone Press,
151 Good Counsel Drive, P.O. Box 669, Mankato, Minnesota 56002.
www.capstonepub.com

Copyright © 2012 by Capstone Press, a Capstone imprint.
All rights reserved.
No part of this publication may be reproduced in whole or in part, or stored in a retrieval system,
or transmitted in any form or by any means, electronic, mechanical, photocopying, recording,
or otherwise, without written permission of the publisher.
For information regarding permission, write to Capstone Press,
151 Good Counsel Drive, P.O. Box 669, Dept. R, Mankato, Minnesota 56002.

Books published by Capstone Press are manufactured with paper
containing at least 10 percent post-consumer waste.

Library of Congress Cataloging-in-Publication Data
Troupe, Thomas Kingsley.
  Fighting a fire, step by step / by Thomas Kingsley Troupe.
    p. cm.—(A+ books. Step-by-step stories)
  ISBN 978-1-4296-6025-9 (library binding)
  1. Fire fighters—Juvenile literature. 2. Fire extinction—Juvenile literature. I. Title.
  HD8039.F5T76 2012
  628.9'25—dc22
                          2011002687

Credits

Shelly Lyons, editor; Ted Williams, designer; Marcie Spence, media researcher; Sarah Schuette, photo stylist;
    Marcy Morin, studio scheduler; Eric Manske, production specialist

Photo Credits

Capstone Studio: Karon Dubke, cover (right and middle), 1, 4-5, 6, 7, 8-9, 9, 10, 11, 12, 13 (top and bottom),
14, 15, 16, 17, 18-19, 20, 21, 24, 25, 26, 27 (top and bottom), 28 (right), 29; Courtesy of Watertown, WI Fire
Department, 27 (middle); Fairbanks Daily News-Miner: John Wagner, 19 (inset); Shutterstock: ehadder, 23
(inset), IntraClique LLC, 13 (middle), Mishella, 22-23, 28 (left), s_oleg, design element, Wally Stemberger,
cover (left)

Note to Parents, Teachers, and Librarians

Step-by-Step Stories is a nonfiction set that teaches sequencing skills along with solid information about the
title subjects. Through fun text and photos, this set supports math and science concepts such as order of
events, relative position words, and ordinal positions. Use the exercise on page 28 to help children practice
their sequencing skills.

Capstone would like to thank the Madelia, Mankato, and New Ulm fire
departments for their assistance with the photos in this book.

Printed in the United States of America in North Mankato, Minnesota.
032011   006110CGF11

Table of Contents

1

Sound the Alarm!

The phone rings at the 911 dispatch center. A scared woman is on the line, shouting. There are flames and smoke in her house! It's time for the fire department to act.

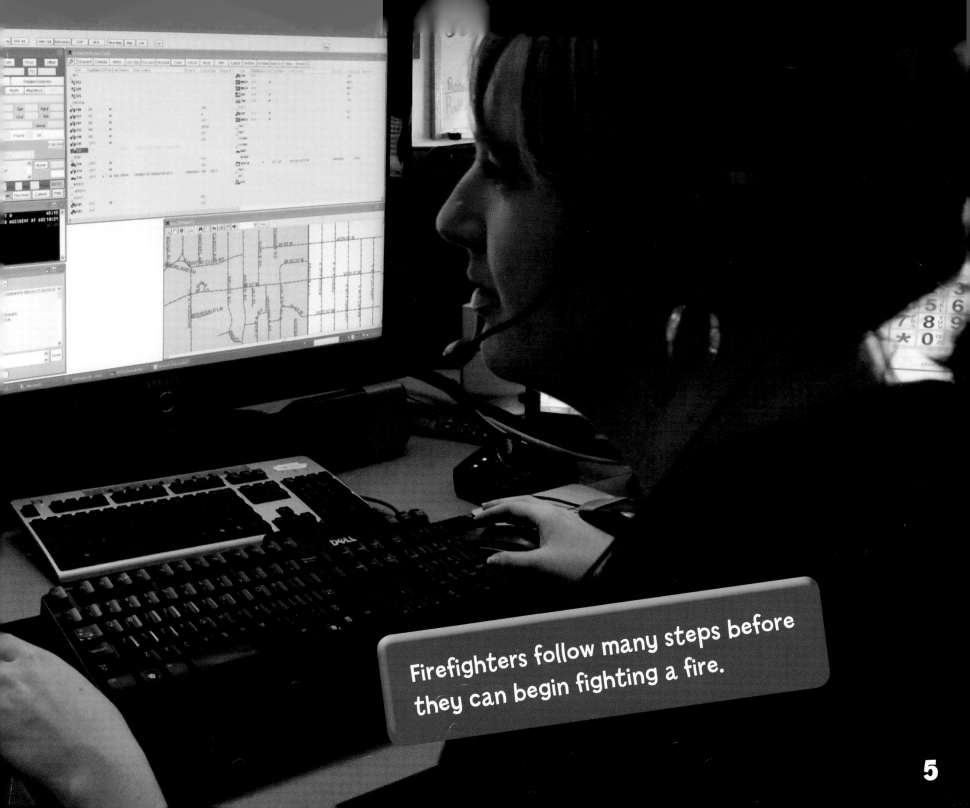

Firefighters follow many steps before they can begin fighting a fire.

First the alarm sounds. A fire alarm can sound at any time. Sleeping firefighters wake up when there's a fire call.

Next the lights come on in the firefighters' rooms. Then a dispatcher tells them about the fire call through a speaker.

Some firefighters don't sleep at the station. Instead, they drive to the station after receiving a fire call at home.

2

Getting Into Gear

The firefighters get dressed in their fire clothes, or turnout gear. Turnout gear is made of special material that doesn't burn easily. It also protects firefighters from heat.

First the firefighters step into boots and pull up their pants. Next they put on coats. And last? The firefighters pull on fireproof hoods. The hoods circle their necks until needed.

The firefighters climb into the truck and go. Then the driver turns on the lights and sirens. He sounds the air horn, warning cars to move out of the way. The firefighters race to the scene.

The seats inside the fire truck have air tanks attached. A firefighter sits down and straps on the tank.

Inside the truck, firefighters put on the air tanks. The air will help them breathe inside a smoky building.

Gathering Tools

3

At the fire, the driver parks the truck near a fire hydrant. Most fire trucks have water in them, but the water can quickly run out. A hydrant will give the truck more water.

One firefighter carries a bag full of tools. The tools will help open the hydrant.

A firefighter runs to the hydrant. First he unscrews the hydrant cover.

Next he flushes out the hydrant.

Then he shuts off the water and hooks up the hose.

13

The engineer controls the water coming in and out. When the hydrant is ready, the engineer opens a valve. The hydrant fills the truck's tank.

The firefighters pull on their masks and turn on the air tanks.

Next they pull hoods over the tops of their heads.

Then they strap on their helmets.

The firefighters bring tools with them to the fire. They bring axes, flashlights, and a radio. They also bring a Halligan bar. This special tool can be used to pry open or break into a locked door.

The most important tool a firefighter brings is the hose. Without water and foam, there's no way to put out the fire.

4

Working as a Team

The firefighters pull the hose from the truck. They will need to work as a team to put out the fire.

If a door to the house is closed, firefighters try the knob first. If it is locked, they'll force the door open with tools.

A firefighting team's priority is safety. First they look for people trapped inside the burning building. The team wants to be sure everyone comes out alive. This means other firefighters too!

Firefighters crawl along the ground where the air is cooler. They search every room.

If they find people, they will bring them out as quickly as possible.

Then firefighters try to put out the fire. They have to work together to use the fire hose. A hose spraying water is hard to hold onto.

A hose that is filled with water is thick and round. It's called a "charged hose."

First the firefighter on the nozzle warns the others. Then he opens the hose. Together the team holds the hose tight. They blast the flames with water and foam.

When the fire is out, the firefighters check for hot spots. A thermal imager can find heat in the walls and ceiling. No one wants a fire to start again.

Once the building is safe, they collect their tools. Then the firefighters disconnect the hoses and unhook the fire hydrant. It's time to drive back to the fire station.

Back at the fire station, the firefighters clean up the tools. They refill the air tanks. More foam and water is added to the truck's tank.

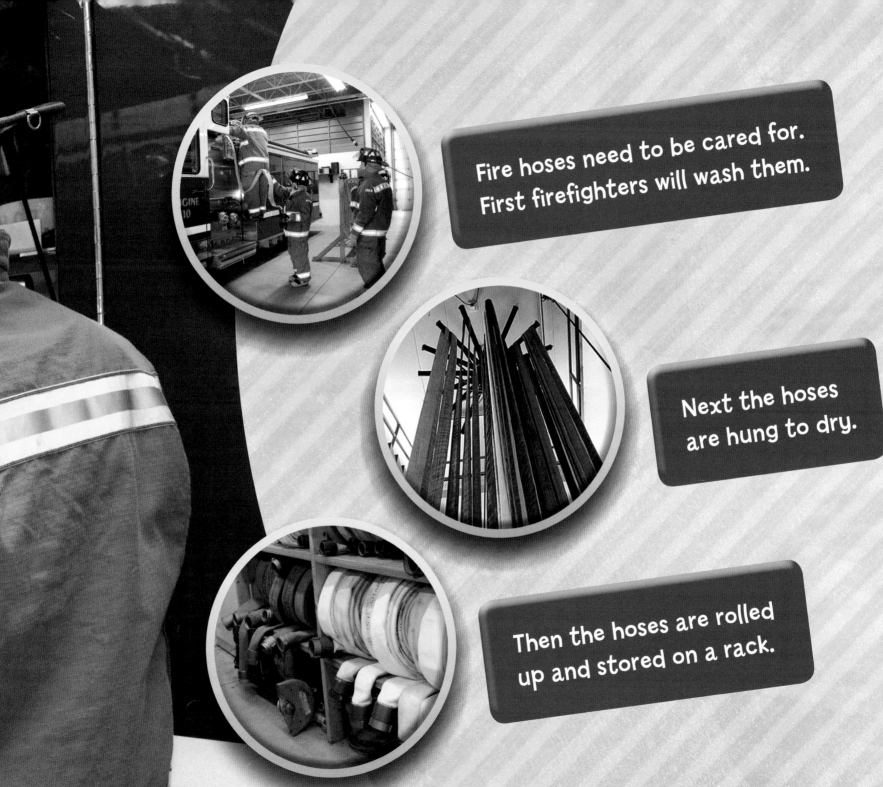

Fire hoses need to be cared for. First firefighters will wash them.

Next the hoses are hung to dry.

Then the hoses are rolled up and stored on a rack.

Now that you've learned the steps in fighting a fire, can you put these pictures in order?

A Spray the fire with water and foam.

B Look for people inside the house.

C Sound the alarm at the station.

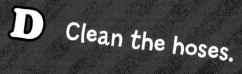**D** Clean the hoses.

Glossary

dispatch center—the place where 911 calls are answered

Halligan bar—a tool used by firefighters and police officers to pry into or strike locked doors

hydrant—a large, upright pipe with a valve that draws water from the city's water supply; hydrants supply water for fighting fires

thermal imager—a tool used by firefighters to search for hot spots in a fire

turnout gear—the special clothing firefighters wear

valve—a moveable part that controls the flow of liquid or gas through a pipe

Read More

Internet Sites

Armentrout, David, and Patricia Armentrout. *The Fire Department.* Our Community. Vero Beach, Fla.: Rourke Publishing, 2009.

Jango-Cohen, Judith. *Fire Trucks.* Mighty Movers. Minneapolis: Lerner Publications, 2011.

Lindeen, Mary. *Fire Trucks.* Mighty Machines. Minneapolis: Bellwether Media, 2007.

FactHound offers a safe, fun way to find Internet sites related to this book. All of the sites on FactHound have been researched by our staff.

Here's all you do:

Visit *www.facthound.com*

Type in this code: 9781429660259

Super-cool stuff! Check out projects, games and lots more at **www.capstonekids.com**

Index